First World War
and Army of Occupation
War Diary
France, Belgium and Germany

25 DIVISION
7 Infantry Brigade
South Staffordshire Regiment
4th Special Reserve Battalion
8 October 1917 - 31 July 1918

WO95/2244/2

The Naval & Military Press Ltd
www.nmarchive.com
Published in association with The National Archives

Published by

The Naval & Military Press Ltd

Unit 10 Ridgewood Industrial Park,

Uckfield, East Sussex,

TN22 5QE England

Tel: +44 (0) 1825 749494

www.naval-military-press.com

www.nmarchive.com

This diary has been reprinted in facsimile from the original. Any imperfections are inevitably reproduced and the quality may fall short of modern type and cartographic standards.

© **Crown Copyright**
Images reproduced by permission of The National Archives, London, England, 2015.

Contents

Document type	Place/Title	Date From	Date To
Heading	WO95/2244-2		
Heading	4th Bn Sth Staffs Regt Oct 1917-July 1918		
War Diary	Bride Camp Canterbury	08/10/1917	08/10/1917
War Diary	Southampton	09/10/1917	10/10/1917
War Diary	Oblinghem	13/10/1917	29/10/1917
War Diary	Bridge Camp Canterbury	08/10/1917	08/10/1917
War Diary	Southampton	09/10/1917	10/10/1917
War Diary	Oblinghem	13/10/1917	29/10/1917
Miscellaneous	Headquarters 7th Infy Bde	03/11/1917	03/11/1917
War Diary	Gorre	10/11/1917	24/11/1917
War Diary	Bethune	27/11/1917	27/11/1917
War Diary	Lillers	28/11/1917	28/11/1917
War Diary	Audingthun	29/11/1917	30/11/1917
War Diary	Audingthun	01/12/1917	02/12/1917
War Diary	Wavrans	04/12/1917	04/12/1917
War Diary	Barastre	06/12/1917	06/12/1917
War Diary	Lagnicourt	11/12/1917	21/12/1917
War Diary	Vaulx	22/12/1917	28/12/1917
War Diary	Camp. (W. Of Vaulx At H.6.a. Central)	01/01/1918	01/01/1918
War Diary	Vaulx	02/01/1918	07/01/1918
War Diary	Lagnicourt	08/01/1918	14/01/1918
War Diary	Camp	15/01/1918	26/01/1918
War Diary	Lagnicourt	27/01/1918	07/02/1918
War Diary	Beugnatre	10/02/1918	10/02/1918
War Diary	Courcelles	27/02/1918	28/02/1918
Heading	4th Battalion South Staffordshire Regiment March 1918		
War Diary	Courcelles Le Comte	01/03/1918	12/03/1918
War Diary	Achietle Grand	12/03/1918	21/03/1918
War Diary	Fremicourt	22/03/1918	24/03/1918
War Diary	Favreuil	24/03/1918	24/03/1918
War Diary	Biefvillers	25/03/1918	31/03/1918
Heading	4th Battalion The South Staffordshire Regiment April 1918		
War Diary	Doullens Neuve Eglise	01/04/1918	10/04/1918
War Diary	Veune Eglise	11/04/1918	30/04/1918
Miscellaneous	HQ 7th Infy Bde	03/06/1918	03/06/1918
War Diary	Steenvoorde	01/05/1918	09/05/1918
War Diary	Arcis-Le-Ponsart	10/05/1918	30/06/1918
Miscellaneous	D.A.G. 3rd Echelon.		
War Diary	In The Field	01/07/1918	31/07/1918
War Diary	4th Battalion, South Staffordshire Regiment.		
Miscellaneous	4th Battalion, South Staffordshire Regiment.		

WO 95/2244/2

26TH DIVISION
7TH INFY BDE

4TH BN STH STAFFS REGT
OCT 1917 — JULY 1918

To 39 DIV 116 BDE

25 Div.

WAR DIARY
or
INTELLIGENCE SUMMARY
(Erase heading not required.)

Army Form C. 2118.

Vol I

4th Bn. North Staffordshire Regiment

Place	Date	Hour	Summary of Events and Information	Remarks and references to Appendices
Bridge Camp CANTERBURY	1917 8. Oct.		The Battalion left by 3 trains for Southampton – 1st Train Regtl. Transport 2.30 am. Right Half Battalion at 5.30 am. & Left Half Battalion & Bn Qrs at 10.30 A.M. There were 44 Officers with the Bn.	
Southampton	9. Oct 1917		The Transport embarked on S.S. Miller and the Battn. marched to a rest Camp about 3 miles out. The weather being too rough for the passage to Havre.	
	10. Oct 1917		The Bn (less the Transport) crossed to Havre during the night of the 10th-11th on S.S. "Archangel". On arrival at Havre, the Battalion marched to No.1 Rest Camp. The weather was very stormy & torrents of rain. The transport arriving the day after.	
OBLINGHEM	13. Oct.		The Battalion was billetted here & joined the 1st Army, 11th Corps, 25th Divn, 7th Brigade. The Billets being about 3½ Miles N of BETHUNE. The Battn. with transport being in one train from Havre.	
"	15. Oct.		The Battalion & Transport were inspected by the G.O.C. 25th Division (Maj. Genl. BAINBRIDGE C.B.). The G.O.C. afterwards addressed the Officers of the Battalion	
	15-29 Oct.		Training was carried on at OBLINGHEM. "A" Coy proceeded to the Divisional Reinforcement Bn. at the FERME DU ROI on the 16th inst. being under training there till the 26th; "B" Coy then took their place.	
	29. Oct.		The Commanding Officer, Adjutant, part of Headquarters, "A" and "C" Coys marched out of OBLINGHEM at 8.30 am. to GORRE, about 3 miles E. of BETHUNE. Headquarters and "C" Coy were then attached to the 3rd Worcester Regt. and "A" Coy to the 10th Cheshire Regt. in the front line of trenches held by the 7th Brigade.	

Chas Charrington Major

WAR DIARY
or
INTELLIGENCE SUMMARY.
(Erase heading not required.)

Army Form C. 2118.

4th South Staffordshire Regt.

Vol I

Place	Date	Hour	Summary of Events and Information	Remarks and references to Appendices
BRIDGE CAMP CANTERBURY	8 Oct. 1917	—	The Battalion left by 3 trains for SOUTHAMPTON – 1st Train Regtl Transport 2-30 a.m. Right Half Battn at 5.30 a.m. & Left half Battn & HQ at 10.30 a.m. There were 44 Officers with the Battn.	Oct '17 to May '18
SOUTHAMPTON	9 Oct 1917		The Transport embarked on S.S. MILLER and the Battn marched to a rest camp about 3 miles out. The weather being too rough for the passage to HAVRE.	
	10 Oct 1917		The Battn (less the transport) crossed to HAVRE during the night of the 10th-11th in S.S. ARCHANGEL. On arrival at HAVRE, the Battalion marched to No 1 Rest camp. The weather was very stormy & torrents of rain. The transport arriving the day after.	
OBLINGHEM	13 Oct		The Battalion was billeted here & joined the 1st Army, 11 Corps, 25 Division, 7th Brigade. The billets being about 3½ miles N of BETHUNE. The Battn with transport being in one train from HAVRE.	
"	15 Oct.		The Battalion & transport were inspected by the G.O.C. 25th Division (MAJ. GENL BAINBRIDGE. CB) The GOC afterwards addressed the Officers of the Battn.	
"	15-29 Oct.		Training was carried on at OBLINGHEM. 'A' Coy proceeded to the Divisional Reinforcement Battn at the FERME du ROI on the 16th inst. being under training there till the 26th; 'B' Coy then took their place.	
"	29 Oct.		The Commanding Officer, Adjutant, part of Headquarters, 'A' & 'C' Coys marched out of OBLINGHEM at 8.30 a.m. to GORRE, about 3 miles E. of BETHUNE. Headquarters and 'C' Coy were then attached to the 3rd Worcester Regt, & 'A' Coy to the 10th Cheshire Regt in the front line of trenches held by the 7th Brigade.	

Geo. Charrington Major
for
LT. COL:
COMMANDING 4TH Bn. SOUTH STAFFORD REGT

Headquarters
7th Infy Bde

Reference your wire O.C. 808
(Re) War Diary (AF.C.2118) attached as requested.
Regret that the original copy has already
been despatched to the Base.
In future, same shall be sent thro' Bde.
H.Q.

K.N. Rennie
7/It Bde
Lt Col
3.11.17

WAR DIARY or INTELLIGENCE SUMMARY

Army Form C. 2118.

(Erase heading not required.)

Place	Date	Hour	Summary of Events and Information	Remarks and references to Appendices
GORRE	10.11.17		2nd in Command and two Coys returned from line on 9th. Whole Bn went up on the 10th and relieved the 8th Bn L.N. LANCS Regt in the line in front of FESTUBERT. A prisoner was taken by B. Coy on 13th.	
"	16.11.17		Bn went into Reserve at GORRE for 6 days. Total Casualties in line :- 9.	
"	22.11.17		Bn. returned to line. A prisoner who surrendered to C. Coy on the 23rd volunteered information concerning a projected raid in front of NO. 14 ISLAND. Front line dispositions were altered but up to the 24th when the Bn was relieved no raid took place.	
"	24.11.17		2nd Lt W.S.J. WILLIAMS wounded during the night by stray bullet. Progressing favourably.	
BETHUNE	27.11.17		Relieved by 8th Bn Manchester Regt, 42nd Division, which has just come down from the coast. Marched and billeted at BETHUNE during night of 27th/28th (8 KILOS)	
LILLERS	28.11.17		Marched to LILLERS and billeted during night of 28th/29th (12 KILOS)	
AUDINGTHUN	29.11.17		Marched to Audingthun. Bn should have been billeted at RECLINGHEM but on arrival at there (25 KILOS) we found that H.Q. & 2 Coys were to be at AUDINGTHUN and the Transport and remaining 2 Coys at COYECQUE, about 3 miles away.	
"	30.11.17		Major C.E.W. CHARRINGTON appointed O.C. COYECQUE Detachment Training areas reconnoitred and reported upon favourably.	

WAR DIARY or INTELLIGENCE SUMMARY.

Army Form C. 2118.

4th Bn. S. Staffs Regt.

Place	Date	Hour	Summary of Events and Information	Remarks and references to Appendices
AUDINGTHUN	Dec. 1st		Orders for move received at 10 p.m.	
AUDINGTHUN	2nd		Battalion proceeded by route march to IVERGNY, where it was billeted for that night and the night of the 3rd/4th, with the exception of C Coy which proceeded to WAVRANS to act as loading party.	
WAVRANS	4th		Battalion entrained in two trains at WAVRANS, travelled all night and detrained at MIRAUMONT on the 5th, whence to BARASTRE by route march on the same day.	
BARASTRE	6th		Battalion remained billeted in huts at BARASTRE until orders were received on the 9th to proceed to LAGNICOURT, to take over from the 12th Bn. West Yorks Regt. in Brigade Support.	
LAGNICOURT	11th		Lt. Col. C.H. Blackall took over the Command from Lt. Col. T.R. STOKOE. D.S.O. who proceeded to ENGLAND prior to employment at a Corps School.	
LAGNICOURT	15th		Remained in support until the 15th when the Battalion relieved the 1st Battn. Wiltshire Regiment in the line, in the Right Subsection of the Brigade front.	
	21st		A considerable amount of wiring was done during the tour, which otherwise was an uneventful one. Total casualties - 3 wounded, all slight.	
VAULX	22nd		On the night of the 21st the Battalion was relieved by the 8th Bn. Border Regt. 75th Infantry Brigade, and proceeded to a hutted and canvas Camp, about a mile West of VAULX, vacated by the 8th Bn. Border Regiment.	
	23rd		Working parties consisting of about 460 other ranks started on the work of burying cable, begun by the 75th Infantry Brigade.	
	26th		Christmas day was held by the Battalion on the 26th, on which date all working parties were cancelled. Men's dinners consisted of Pork and Vegetables, plum puddings, and beer. All officers Messed in one Hut.	
	28th		A Shell amongst one of the working parties killed 2 and wounded 2/Lt. DOLMAN and 3 others.	

WAR DIARY or INTELLIGENCE SUMMARY

Army Form C. 2118.

Instructions regarding War Diaries and Intelligence Summaries are contained in F. S. Regs., Part II. and the Staff Manual respectively. Title pages will be prepared in manuscript.

(Erase heading not required.)

4th S. Staffs

Vol 4

Place	Date	Hour	Summary of Events and Information	Remarks and references to Appendices
Camp. (W. of VAULX at H 6.a. central)	1-1-18		Battalion in Divisional Reserve.	
VAULX	2-1-18 to 7-1-18		Battalion moved up into Brigade Reserve in VAULX. Working parties supplied daily.	
LAGNICOURT	8-1-18 to 14-1-18		Relieved the 8th Bn. Border Regt. in the Line. Very cold weather until last few days when thaw set in. Two prisoners taken by C Company on 11th inst. Casualties Nil. 2nd Lt. N.AMIS proceeded to ENGLAND for attachment to M.G.C. 14-1-18	
Camp.	15-1-18 to 26-1-18		Battalion moved back into Divisional Reserve on night of 14th/15th Jan. Working parties found for work on VAULX - MORCHIES Line and worthy of HIRONDELLE VALLEY. on 22nd 2nd Lt. G.H.N.LAW proceeded to ENGLAND for attachment to M.G.C. 18-1-18 One party working by day was shelled and suffered casualties (1 killed, 1 died of wounds, 6 wounded and 1 wounded (at duty))	
LAGNICOURT	27-1-18		Moved up into Brigade Support on night of 26/27th and relieved 8th Bn. The Border Regt.	
"	29-1-18		One man employed at Brigade Instructional Platoon wounded by Bomb from Aeroplane	
"	30-1-18		Two men accidentally wounded by explosion of German Grenade	
"	31-1-18		2nd Lt DAVIDSON proceeded to ENGLAND for attachment to R.F.C.	

C W Beckall Lt Col
Commandg 4th Bn South Stafford Regt

WAR DIARY or INTELLIGENCE SUMMARY

Army Form C. 2118.

4th Bn. S. Staffs Regt.

Vol 5

Place	Date	Hour	Summary of Events and Information	Remarks and references to Appendices
LAGNICOURT	1-2-18		The Battalion relieved the 1st Bn. Wiltshire Regt. in the Right Subsection of the line (QUÉANT Sector). Right front: A Coy. Left front: D Coy. Right Support: B Coy. Left Support: C Coy.	
"	2-2-18		5 men wounded (at duty) by explosion of .77 m.m. shell.	
"	4-2-18		Increased enemy shelling especially in neighbourhood of CORN ALLEY.	
"	5-2-18		From 4 a.m. to 6.30 a.m. there was considerable hostile shell fire, the enemy apparently suspecting attack started to fire on his S.O.S. lines and worked back to the Support Battalion firing very erratically the whole time. Casualties nil. except for 1 Killed by chance shell about 9 a.m.	
"	6-2-18		A destructive shoot on enemy defences between QUÉANT and PRONVILLE from 2 p. to 2.15 p. was carried out by our artillery for the benefit of a party of Serbian officers.	
"	7-2-18		Battalion relieved by 8th Bn. Border Regt. and returned to FLOODY Camp.	
BEUGNATRE	10-2-18		Battalion relieved by 2nd Bn. York and Lancs Regt. and proceeded to No. 2 Camp COURCELLES.	
COURCELLES	27-2-18		Company and Platoon training carried out during this time, special attention being paid to Musketry and the use of Tumplines. The Transport was inspected by the B.G.C. on the 27th and highly complimented on their turn out.	R.
	28-2-18		Practice Alarm was held under Battalion arrangements.	5.

C. Blackburn Lt. Col.
Comdg. 4th Bn. South Stafford Regt.

25th Division.

7th Infantry Brigade.

WAR DIARY

4th BATTALION

SOUTH STAFFORDSHIRE REGIMENT

MARCH 1918

4th South Staffordshire Regt.

WAR DIARY or INTELLIGENCE SUMMARY.
(Erase heading not required.)

Army Form C. 2118.

4th Bn. S. Staffs Regt.

Vol 6

Place	Date	Hour	Summary of Events and Information	Remarks and references to Appendices
COURCELLES LE COMTE	MARCH 1st to 12th		In No. 2 Camp. Training carried on.	
ACHIET LE GRAND	12th to 21st		Battalion marched to RITZ Camp, ACHIET LE GRAND. Training carried on.	
	21st	Noon	The Battalion under Command of Lt. Col. C.W. BLACKALL marched to FREMICOURT. "B" team remained behind, and proceeded to Corps Reinforcement Camp at ACHIET LE PETIT.	
		11.30pm	Battalion went up and dug in behind the Army line on left of the road behind between BEUGNY and FREMICOURT.	
FREMICOURT	22nd		Remained in this line during the day.	
	23rd	3pm	"C" & "D" Coys. formed a defensive flank on the left, "A" & "B" remaining in their position. At night "C" & "D" returned to support "A" & "B" who were still in the Army line, which had now become the front line.	
	24th	2am	Relieved by battalion of 62nd Division; retired to position between FREMICOURT and BEUGNATRE and dug in there.	
FAVREUIL		3pm	Reorganized in Sunken road just N of Railway line.	
		6pm	Took up position in trench W. of BAPAUME - ARRAS Road and just S. of MONUMENT.	
		8pm	Retired across main road & dug in 400 yds due E. of BIEFVILLERS.	
BIEFVILLERS	25th	9am	Lt. Col. C.W. BLACKALL killed. Battalion retired to a line between	

WAR DIARY or **INTELLIGENCE SUMMARY.**

Army Form C. 2118.

(Erase heading not required.)

Place	Date	Hour	Summary of Events and Information	Remarks and references to Appendices
BIEFVILLERS	March 25th	9am	between GREVILLERS and BIEFVILLERS. Retired in afternoon to line which was being dug by 7th Inf. Bde. between ACHIET LE GRAND and ACHIET LE PETIT.	
		10pm	Marched back to BUCQUOY.	
	26th	2am	Marched to GOMMECOURT.	
		4am	Took up position in GOMMECOURT WOOD facing HEBUTERNE.	
		6pm	Took up fresh position near LA BRAYELLE FARM. Lt. Col. L.H.K. FINCH DSO. to over Command.	
	27th	1am	Marched to COIGNEUX.	
		2pm	Marched to PONCHVILLERS.	
	28th	8am	Left the P. of War Camp and marched to HALLOY near CANAPLES. Stayed there two days.	
	30th	11.30pm	Marched to DOULLENS.	
	31st	10am	Entrained and travelled to GODEVAERSVELDE. By lorries to SHANKSHILL CAMP at NEUVE EGLISE.	

V. A. Rhodes
Lt. Col.
Cdg 4th Bn. SOUTH STAFFORDSHIRE

25th Division.
7th Infantry Brigade.

WAR DIARY

4th BATTALION

THE SOUTH STAFFORDSHIRE REGIMENT

APRIL 1918.

WAR DIARY
or
INTELLIGENCE SUMMARY
(Erase heading not required.)

Army Form 2118.

4 Bn S Staffs

Place	Date 1918	Hour	Summary of Events and Information	Remarks and references Appendic
			Battalion entrained 9.30 am for GODEWAERSVELDE detrained 5pm and conveyed by bus to NEUVE EGLISE.	
Neuve Eglise	April 1		Inspection of 7th Infy Bde by Genl Plumer at 5pm. Bn moved into the line at PLOEGSTREET WOOD in support to 10 Cheshires on right & 1st Wilts on left. Disposition on front line. Battalion:- A Coy at Bakery, B Coy in Ploegsteert Wood, C Coy in Avenue Farm, D Coy in Catacombs Hyde Pk Corner.	
	2			
	3		Capt L.J. Kersey M.C. took over command of B Coy from Capt A H Hutt who assumed duties of Adjutant.	
	4		Reconnaissance of 7th Bde Area by all Officers & NCOs preparatory to Bn moving into front line. 1st L.G. Moncrieff rejoined Unit from L.G. Course. Reinforcements arrived.	
	5		Lt. A.B. Miller proceeded to Transport Lines to instruct L.G. Classes. Strength in trenches reduced to 110 per Coy. Surplus returned to Transport Lines. At dusk (7.45pm) the Battalion relieved the 1st Wilts in left sub-section. Dispositions of Battalion:- A Coy at WATCHFUL POST, TILLEUL FM & LA POTERIE, B Coy in GREY FM RESERVE. C Coy at AVENUE FM. D Coy in front line.	
	6		Lt. F.R. Laver rejoined B Coy from leave.	
	7		B Coy less 1½ pltns relieved A Coy in WATCHFUL POST TILLEUL FM & LA POTERIE. A Coy went back to Catacombs at Hyde Park Corner. C Coy relieved D Coy in front line. 2/Lt O.H. Mason took command of C Coy. 1½ platoons of B Coy remained at GREY FM RES	
	8		2 sections B Coy under 2/Lt A.E. Collins moved from GREY FM RES to ANTINK TRENCH in afternoon and in evening to WATCHFUL POST. 2 sections of B Coy to USEFUL SPOT (Mr Laver). During the day and on patrol in the black area.	
	9			
	10		Enemy attack opened about 3.30am by heavy shelling over the whole of the Battalion area. At 5.30am he opened his barrage on front & support lines lasting about an hour, then lengthened to Reserve on about line of GREY FM. B Coy in front line wiped out. 2/Lts W. HIREY & A.P. WALKER missing. 10th Platoon B Coy withdrew to WATCHFUL POST owing to enemy shelling. 11th Platoon B Coy 1st sects platoon moved forward but was unable to occupy positions. 11 Laver wounded & missing. No Cheshires on left, 10 Cheshires on right having withdrawn allowed moved to withdraw from WATCHFUL POST. Battalion withdrew to Catacombs at 2pm, order to reoccupy old position received 5pm.	

Place	Date	Hour	Summary of Events and Information	Remarks and references to Appendices
NEUVE EGLISE	April 10		Boch attacked 7 pm. Grey Farm garrison stood fast, remainder of Bn withdrew to Hill 63 position. Relieved, Bn withdrew to Neuve Eglise.	
	April 11		Battalion reorganised and took up outpost duty. Afternoon marched to Bailleul and took up outpost position.	
	April 12		12.30 am marched to Crucifix Corner, occupied line of trenches. Enemy attacked about 7 am & at 7 pm unsuccessfully both cases.	
	April 13		Front line reinforced by details of 6th & 34th Div. Boches attacked 5.30 pm until dusk. Slight advance.	
	April 14		Relieved 4.30 am 9th Norfolks, moved to Loore Château at 4 pm.	
	April 15		At noon moved to MONT NOIR, dug in MOLHOEK Fm. French moved up thro' us and attacked before dawn.	
	— 16		Heavy shelling of woods & slopes of MT. NOIR by enemy.	
	— 17		Battalion returned to billets MT. KOKEREELE.	
	— 18		Seven new Officers joined Bn.	
	— 20		Moved to Sheffield Camp.	
	— 21		Major F. Stewart MC. took over Command of Bn.	
	— 24		Reorganising Bn.	
	— 25		Bn moved forward, bad weather, arrived Reninghelst at 5 p. stayed till dark.	
	— 26		Crossed the open by platoons east Reninghelst — Lt. COTTE and attacked at 3 am. Battalion reached Kemmel village, little opposition, had to withdraw to old trenches owing to the flanks being open. Major Stewart Killed.	
	— 27		Battalion were relieved by Loyal North Lancs and moved to some huts on the MILLE RENNES OUDERDOM Rd. Major Cranington took Command.	
	— 28		In trenches on RENNINGHELST — LA COTTE Road.	
	— 29		Major Morgan (SWB) took Command of Bn. MONT ROUGE & SCHERPENBERG reported in hands of enemy. Battalion formed as defensive flank. Report contradicted & moved back to NEWCASTLE CAMP.	
	— 30		All quiet throughout the day.	

C.O. 4th Bn SOUTH STAFFORDSHIRE REGIMENT.

H Qrs
7th L'pools
4th Bde
10

Herewith War Diary of
4th Bn South Staffordshire
Regiment for the month
of May.

[signature]
Lt. Col.
Comdg 4th South Staffords. Regt.

6/
/18

WAR DIARY
or
INTELLIGENCE SUMMARY.

Army Form C. 2118.

Place	Date	Hour	Summary of Events and Information	Remarks and references to Appendices
Steenvoorde	May 1st		Capt. Hewetson and 3 officers joined Transport Lines.	
	2		Officers joined Bn at KEMMEL	
	4		Battalion relieved by the 153 French Infy Regt and proceeded to Transport Lines	
	5		Marched to BISSEZEELE. reorganising etc.	
	8		Marched to REXPOEDE	
	9		Entrained for SOISSONS Area.	
ARCIS-LE-PONSART	10		Detrained at SERZY and marched to ARCIS-LE-PONSART	
	11 to 22		Training	
	23		Marched to MONTIGNY-SUR-VESLE	
	24		Cleaning up etc	
	25		Fire broke out in Officers Quarters 2/Lt. J.W. Shorry burnt to death.	
	26		Bn received orders to be ready to move off at a moment's notice after 8pm. At 12 M.N. Bn moved to a position south-west of GOYENCOURT	
	27		Battn moved forward to a position SW of CORMICY after severe fighting withdrew to PEVY	
	28		Moved forward to take up a position N of PEVY. The position	

WAR DIARY or INTELLIGENCE SUMMARY.

Army Form C. 2118.

Place	Date	Hour	Summary of Events and Information	Remarks and references to Appendices
			was occupied by the Boch and it was necessary to withdraw to the high grounds SE of PROUILLY. Then withdrew to a position about 2 Kilos east of JONCHERY-REIMS Road.	
	29th		During evening the Bosch was getting round the flanks and it was necessary to withdraw to SAPICOURT road and again from there to ROSNAY and on to high ground S of ROSNAY. Orders were received to withdraw from the line and marched to MERY-PREMECY. Casualties to Officers 6 wounded 1 wounded & missing and 4 missing. O Ranks. 10 Killed 92 Wounded 63 missing	
	30		During the night Bn marched to MARFAUX about 7 Kilos. At 11.30 am Bn marched to FORÊT D'EPERNAY 20 Kilos.	
	31		Bn marched to SOULIERS 14 Kilos.	

June 3/18.

H.A. Hawkins 2nd Lt
for Lt. Col.
Comdg 4th

WAR DIARY
or
INTELLIGENCE SUMMARY.
(Erase heading not required.)

Army Form C. 2118.

4 S Staff R

Place	Date	Hour	Summary of Events and Information	Remarks and references to Appendices
	June 1	-	Battalion marched from SOULIÈRES to transport at BEAUNAY.	
	2	-	Church Parade. Composite company of 150 men formed under Lieut. H. Guiton and moved to LOISY.	
	3 & 4		Inspections.	
	5		Composite Company returned.	
	6.		Another composite company of 250 men formed under Capt. Bates and formed with Cheshires and Wilts the 75 Composite Battalion commanded by Lt. Col. R. J. Morris D.S.O. Composite Battalion marched to ETOGES and went up the line from there in busses.	
	7.		Comp. Coy rested in the wood S.W. of NANTIEUL.	
	8.		Comp. Coy went into reserve in the Bois de COURTON.	
	9.		Comp. Coy relieved S.W.Bs & 1/6th Cheshires in front line in B d'ECLISES. Transport left BEAUNAY for line and remainder of Battalion to REUVES.	
	10			
	11.		Comp Coy relieved by S.W.Bs and moved to support in the	

WAR DIARY or INTELLIGENCE SUMMARY.

Army Form C. 2118.

(Erase heading not required.)

Place	Date	Hour	Summary of Events and Information	Remarks and references to Appendices
			S. of the wood.	
	12		Comp. Coy relieved by 3/25th Bn in the line E of CHANTERINE. M. Lt Col. R.J Morris DSO relieved by Major Bridges.	
	15		Comp. Coy relieved by Cheshire Coy and moved into reserve in the Bois de COURTON.	
	17.		Bn moved to CORROY. 3/25th Comp. Coy relieved by Italians.	
	18.		Comp Coy entrained at GERMAINE and detrained at FERE CHAMPENOISE and marched to Bn at CORROY. Bn marched to GOURGANCON.	
	19 & 20.		Inspection.	
	21.		Two Comp Coys of 350 OR formed under Lt. Gillender and moved to PÉAS.	
	22		Remainder of Bn moved to OEUVY	
	23.		Church Parade.	
	24.		Bn marched to MAILLY-LE-CAMP.	

WAR DIARY or INTELLIGENCE SUMMARY.

Army Form C. 2118.

Place	Date	Hour	Summary of Events and Information	Remarks and references to Appendices
	25.		Training	
	26.		Battalion entrained at MAILLY at 2 am.	
	27.		Bn detrained at MARESQUEL at 12 midday & marched to CRÉVY.	
	28.		Training.	
	29.		Training.	
	30.		Church Parade.	

H.J. Norris Lt. Col.
Comdg 4th South Staffords. Regt.

D.A.G.
3rd Echelon.

4

July 1918.

Herewith original copy of War Diary for

[signature]
Lieut Colonel.
Comdg. 4th South Staffordshire Regt.

WAR DIARY
or
INTELLIGENCE SUMMARY.
(Erase heading not required.)

Army Form C. 2118.

4TH BATTALION,
SOUTH STAFFS
REGIMENT.
No. 238.
Date 1-8-18

Place	Date	Hour	Summary of Events and Information	Remarks and references to Appendices
In the Field	July 1st 1918		Bn. left CRÉQUY & marched to EMBRY	
	2nd		Lt. FAIRY joined the Bn. & commenced duties as Quartermaster	
	9th		Bn. left EMBRY at 6.30 am & marched to HESDIN entraining there at 2.15 p.m.	
	10th		Detrained at 2 am at PONT REMY. Bn. spent night on the station & then marched to LIMERCOURT	
	11th		Bn. formed into a Training Cadre of 10 Officers & 57 O.R. All other Officers & men joined the remainder of the batt'n, forming No. 3 Composite Bn, at DOUDELAINVILLE	
	12th		Tg. Cadre moved to HUPPY	
	14th		Capt. R.D. OLDHAM M.C. rejoined the battalion.	
	18th		Officers & O.R. at DOUDELAINVILLE proceed to the base.	
	19th		Cadre embussed at HUPPY & moved to ROUXMESNIL. Officers and other ranks surplus to training cadre struck off strength.	
	30th		2nd Lt. H. THOMAS proceeded on leave to England. 2nd Lt. C. BATES D.S.O. M.C. D.C.M. returned from leave.	
	31st		Capt. A.B. MILLER D.S.O. M.C. rejoined.	

Lt. Col.
Comdg 4th South Staffords R.

4th BATTALION, SOUTH STAFFORDSHIRE REGIMENT.

Appendix.

IN THE FIELD.

1918

July

1st — Bn left CREQUY & marched to WIBRY.

2nd — Lt W-H-H FAIRY joined the Bn. & commenced duties as Quartermaster.

9th — Bn left WIBRY at 6.30 a.m. & marched to HESDIN entraining there at 2.15 p.m.

10th — Detrained at 1 a.m. at PONT REMY. Bn. spent night on the station & then marched to LIERCOURT.

11th — Bn. formed into a Training Cadre of 10 officers & 57 O.R. All other officers & men joined the remainder of the battn, forming No.3 Composite Bn. at DOUDELAINVILLE

12th — Tn.Cadre moved to HUPPY.

14th — Capt. R.D. OLDHAM M.C. rejoined the battalion.

18th — Officers & O.R. at DOUDELAINVILLE proceed to the base.

19th — Cadre embussed at HUPPY & moved to ROUXMESNIL. Officers and other ranks surplus to training cadre struck off strength.

30th — 2nd Lt H. THOMAS proceeded on leave to England. 2nd Lt C. BATES D.S.O., M.C., D.C.M. returned from leave.

31st — Capt. A.B. MILLER D.S.O., M.C. rejoined.

R.J. MORRIS.
Lt.Col.
Commdg. 4th South Staffords Regt.

4th BATTALION. SOUTH STAFFORDSHIRE REGIMENT.

Appendix.

1918
July

IN THE FIELD.

1st	Bn left GENECHY & marched to HERRY.
2nd	Bn left HERRY & commenced duties as quartermaster.
9th	Lt ---- FAIRY joined the Bn. & marched to HERDIN entraining there at 2.15 p.m.
10th	Bn left HERRY at 6.30 a.m. & marched to HERDIN entraining there at 2.15 p.m.
11th	Detrained at 1 a.m. at FORT REMY. Bn. spent night on the station & then marched to LINGHOURT.
12th	Bn. formed into a Training Cadre of 19 officers & 57 O.R. All other officers & men joined the remainder of the battn. forming No.3 Composite Bn. at BOUBELAIMVILLE
14th	Tn.Cadre moved to HUFFY.
18th	Capt. R.D. GLUMAN M.C. rejoined the battalion.
19th	Officers & O.R. at BOUBELAIMVILLE proceed to the base.
30th	Cadre embussed at HUFFY & moved to HOUESEILL. Officers and other ranks surplus to training cadre struck off strength.
31st	2nd Lt H. THOMAS proceeded on leave to England. 2nd Lt C. BATES R.S.O., M.C., D.C.M. returned from leave. Capt. A.J. MILLER D.S.O., M.C. rejoined.

R.J. MORRIS.
Lt.Col.
Commdg. 4th South Staffords Regt.

4th BATTALION, SOUTH STAFFORDSHIRE REGIMENT.

Appendix.

1918
July

IN THE FIELD.

1st	Bn left CREQUY & marched to EMBRY.
2nd	Lt ---- FAIRY joined the Bn. & commenced duties as quartermaster.
9th	Bn left EMBRY at 6.30 a.m. & marched to HESDIN entraining there at 2.15 P.M.
10th	Detrained at 1 a.m. at PONT REMY. Bn. spent night on the station & then marched to LINESCOURT.
11th	Bn. formed into a Training Cadre of 10 officers & 57 O.R. All other officers & men joined the remainder of the batt, forming No.3 Composite Bn. at DOUDELAINVILLE
12th	Tn.Cadre moved to HUPPY.
14th	Capt. R.D. OLDHAM M.C. rejoined the battalion.
18th	Officers & O.R. at DOUDELAINVILLE proceed to the base.
19th	Cadre embussed at HUPPY & moved to ROUENSNIL. Officers and other ranks surplus to training cadre struck off strength.
30th	2nd Lt H. THOMAS proceeded on leave to England. 2nd Lt C. BATES D.S.O., M.C., D.C.M. returned from leave.
31st	Capt. A.B. MILLER D.S.O., M.C. rejoined.

R.J. MORRIS.
Lt.Col.
Commdg. 4th South Staffords Regt.

www.ingramcontent.com/pod-product-compliance
Lightning Source LLC
Chambersburg, PA
CBHW081250170426
43191CB00037B/2105